LIBRARY OF
AWESOME ANIMALS

PRAYING MANTIS

By Rachel Rose

BEARPORT
PUBLISHING

Minneapolis, Minnesota

Credits

Cover and title page, © Simon002/iStock and © EAKARAT BUANOI/Shutterstock; 3, © Simon002/iStock; 4–5, © Kristina Postnikova/Shutterstock; 7, © monster_code/iStock; 8, © TLF/Shutterstock; 9, © valio84sl/iStock; 10, © Juan Francisco Moreno Gamez/iStock; 11, ©monster_code/Adobe Stock; 12, © Paul Looyen/Shutterstock; 13, © Andrew Waugh/iStock; 15, © artas/iStock; 17, © The Nature Guy/Adobe Stock; 18, © Mohamed Haddad/iStock; 19, © Andriy Nekrasov/iStock; 20, © Akchamczuk/iStock; 21, © monster_code/iStock; 22L, ©Ville Heikkinen/iStock; 22R, © oleg7799/iStock; 23, © monster_code/iStock.

Bearport Publishing Company Product Development Team

President: Jen Jenson; Director of Product Development: Spencer Brinker; Managing Editor: Allison Juda; Associate Editor: Naomi Reich; Associate Editor: Tiana Tran; Art Director: Colin O'Dea; Designer: Kayla Eggert; Product Development Assistant: Owen Hamlin

STATEMENT ON USAGE OF GENERATIVE ARTIFICIAL INTELLIGENCE

Bearport Publishing remains committed to publishing high-quality nonfiction books. Therefore, we restrict the use of generative AI to ensure accuracy of all text and visual components pertaining to a book's subject. See BearportPublishing.com for details.

Library of Congress Cataloging-in-Publication Data

Names: Rose, Rachel, 1968- author.
Title: Praying mantis / by Rachel Rose.
Description: Minneapolis, Minnesota : Bearport Publishing Company, [2025] | Series: Library of awesome animals | Includes bibliographical references and index.
Identifiers: LCCN 2023059631 (print) | LCCN 2023059632 (ebook) | ISBN 9798892320245 (library binding) | ISBN 9798892325028 (paperback) | ISBN 9798892321495 (ebook)
Subjects: LCSH: Praying mantis--Juvenile literature.
Classification: LCC QL505.9.M35 R67 2025 (print) | LCC QL505.9.M35 (ebook) | DDC 595.7/27--dc23/eng/20240129
LC record available at https://lccn.loc.gov/2023059631
LC ebook record available at https://lccn.loc.gov/2023059632

For more information, write to Bearport Publishing, 5357 Penn Avenue South, Minneapolis, MN 55419.

Contents

AWESOME

Praying Mantises!

A praying mantis slowly turns its head and spies its **prey**. *POUNCE!* The **insect** quickly jumps in for the kill. Fast and deadly, praying mantises are awesome!

PRAYING MANTISES ARE THE ONLY INSECTS THAT CAN TURN THEIR HEADS WITHOUT MOVING THEIR BODIES.

It's in the Name

Praying mantises have long, thin bodies and six skinny legs. Many have two pairs of wings and can fly. However, the most iconic part of their look is their two front legs, bent and folded close together just under their triangular heads. This makes the insects look as though they're praying, which is how they got their name!

FEMALE MANTISES ARE BIGGER THAN MALES. THE FEMALES USUALLY CAN'T FLY BECAUSE THEY ARE TOO HEAVY!

Many Mantis Homes

There are more than 2,000 **species** of praying mantises. They are found in different **habitats** around the world. Many species live in warm rainforests where there are lots of plants. Some make their homes up in trees, while others live closer to the ground in low bushes and leaves.

SOME PRAYING MANTIS SPECIES ARE FOUND IN DESERTS AND GRASSLANDS.

Hiding in Plain Sight

Wherever they live, these insects are big. Most grow between 2 and 5 inches (5 and 13 cm) long. But thanks to their ability to **camouflage**, they can be almost impossible to spot! Some species are brown or green with leaf-shaped bodies. Others, such as orchid mantises, have bodies that are a similar color and shape to the flowers they sit on.

CONEHEAD MANTISES HAVE SPIKES ON THEIR HEADS AND THIN BODIES THAT LOOK LIKE TWIGS.

Eyes on the Prize

Praying mantises are excellent hunters. Their camouflage helps them stay hidden in their surroundings while they keep an eye out for their next meal. In fact, these insects have 5 eyes and can see movement up to 60 feet (18 m) away. For the most part, they munch on other insects. Some species also hunt bigger animals, such as hummingbirds and mice.

PRAYING MANTISES HAVE TWO LARGE EYES ON THEIR FACES AND THREE SMALLER ONES ON TOP OF THEIR HEADS.

Pounce and Pin

To hunt, mantises hold their bodies still and slowly turn their heads more than 180 degrees to look for their next **victim**. Once they've spied their prey, the insects strike quickly. They pounce with lightning speed. Mantises pin the meal down with their strong front legs. Spikes on their legs weave together like a cage, trapping the prey. Dinner is served. *CRUNCH!*

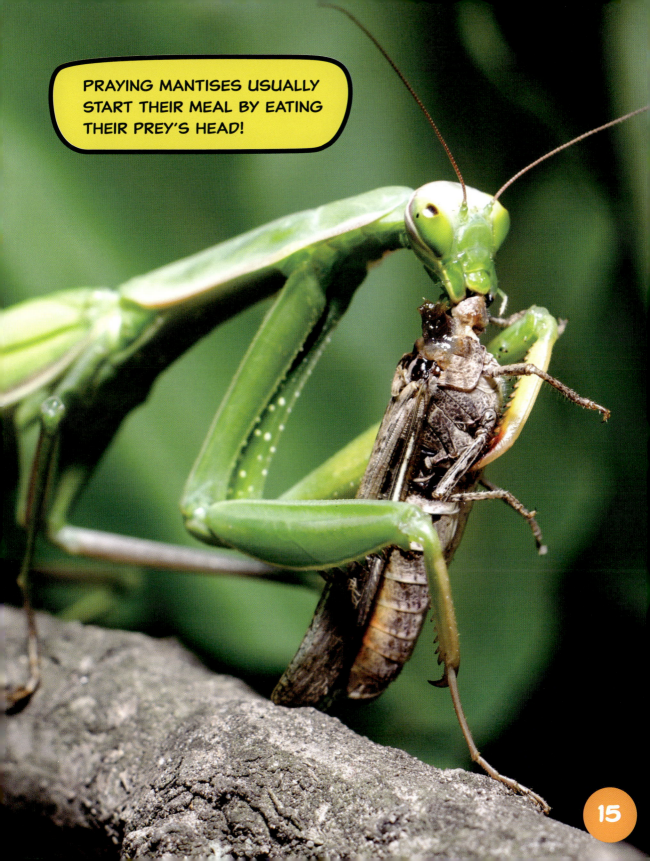

PRAYING MANTISES USUALLY START THEIR MEAL BY EATING THEIR PREY'S HEAD!

Big and Bold

Sometimes, camouflage keeps mantises safe from **predators**. However, the big insects don't back down from a fight if they are spotted. Praying mantises stand on their back legs while raising their wings and front legs. They do this to make their bodies look even bigger in hopes it might scare the attacker away.

FROGS, LIZARDS, BIRDS, AND SOME SPIDERS ATTACK PRAYING MANTISES.

Watch Out, Pops!

Praying mantises usually **mate** in the fall. This can be a dangerous time for males. Sometimes, a female mantis eats her partner. *OUCH!* A big meal like this gives her plenty of energy to make eggs. She lays her eggs in a foamlike case that hardens very quickly. Soon after, the mother mantis dies.

A PRAYING MANTIS CASE CAN HAVE UP TO 400 EGGS.

A female mantis eating her partner

Hungry Nymphs

The eggs of most mantis species hatch in the spring. The babies, called nymphs (NIMFS), look like tiny versions of the adults. Nymphs start searching for something to eat right away. But if they can't find enough food, they may eat each other. **YIKES!** The young nymphs grow and **molt** a few times before becoming adults by summer.

PRAYING MANTISES USUALLY LIVE FOR ABOUT ONE YEAR.

PRAYING MANTISES ARE AWESOME!
LET'S LEARN EVEN MORE ABOUT THEM.

Kind of animal: Praying mantises are insects. Like all insects, they have six legs, three main body parts, and a hard covering.

More hiding insects: Many insects use camouflage. Walkingstick insects have long, thin bodies that look like twigs.

Size: One of the largest praying mantises ever found was almost 8 in. (20 cm) long. That's about the size of a banana.

PRAYING MANTISES AROUND THE WORLD

Arctic Ocean

EUROPE

ASIA

NORTH AMERICA

Pacific Ocean

Atlantic Ocean

AFRICA

Pacific Ocean

N
W E
S

SOUTH AMERICA

Indian Ocean

AUSTRALIA

Southern Ocean

ANTARCTICA

WHERE PRAYING MANTISES LIVE

camouflage the colors and markings on an animal's body that help it blend in with its surroundings

female a praying mantis that can lay eggs

habitats places in nature where animals live

insect a small animal that has six legs, three main body parts, and a hard covering

males praying mantises that cannot lay eggs

mate to come together in order to have young

molt to shed an outer layer of skin

predators animals that hunt and kill other animals for food

prey an animal that is hunted and eaten by another animal

species groups that animals are divided into according to similar characteristics

victim an animal that is attacked or killed by another animal

Index

Read More

Downs, Kieran. *Praying Mantis vs. Black Widow Spider (Animal Battles).* Minneapolis: Bellwether Media, Inc., 2022.

Markle, Sandra. *Praying Mantises: An Augmented Reality Experience (Creepy Crawlers in Action: Augmented Reality).* Minneapolis: Lerner Publishing, 2021.

Learn More Online

1. Go to **www.factsurfer.com** or scan the QR code below.
2. Enter "**Praying Mantis**" into the search box.
3. Click on the cover of this book to see a list of websites.

About the Author

Rachel Rose writes books for kids and teaches yoga. Her favorite animal for all time is her dog, Sandy.